Color Me Alice:

Wonderland, Hats and a Looking Glass

Dale Ann Clancy

www.TangledEnchantmentStudio.com

Please use the pages at the back of the book as bleed through test pages. If you find that your pens, markers or water colors are bleeding through simply put a sheet of paper or cardboard behind it, as each image is printed on a single sheet.

To my grandpa Clancy... Who was such a loving grandfather and important influence in my life. He was so funny, genuine and taught me how to find joy in the little things and to celebrate my inner child. I dedicate this book to your sweet memory.

Words cannot express the gratitude I have for my amazing, talented, professional, beautiful and dedicated cast. For enduring the early morning call times (but I always had your favorite donuts and coffee), multiple costume fittings, make up sittings and general production shenanigans, you are rock stars, all. From the bottom of this red head's heart, I say thank you and Big Smooch!

Cast List

- Alexander – Playing Card
- Ashlee – Alice
- Bryan – White King
- Caiden – Playing Card
- Cat – Red Queen
- Charlotte – White Rabbit
- Claudia - Larkspur
- Gregg – Mad Hatter
- Helena - Rose
- Jeffery – March Hare
- Kara C. – Tweedledee
- Kara N. - Daisy
- Krista - Tweedledum
- Luna - Dinah
- Michele - Dormouse
- Misty – Cheshire Cat
- Monet – Tiger Lilly
- Nikolette - Violet
- Scottlyn – White Queen
- Stephen – Man in the White Paper Suit
- Teresa - Jabberwocky
- Zouhair – Red King

Photographer/Art Director/Queen of Everything/Redhead Extraordinaire
   Dale Ann Clancy

My Amazing Photo Assistant/Gaffer/Grip
   Terry Whittaker

Photo Assistant
   Mark Burrow

Location Scout God
   Mark Burrow

Hair/Makeup/Set Design Styling/Costume Designer/Stylist
   Dale Clancy

FX Makeup/Wings/Head Dress for the Jabberwocky
   Katie Lombard

Specialized Prop Creation
   Desiree Rahill from Over the Top Photo Op' Props Sarasota FL
      Oversized Teapot (Pg. 37)
      Hedgehog Croquete Ball (Pg. 51)

Stylist/Prop Manager/Assistants
   Cat
   Corinna
   Dawn
   Katie

Makeup Assistants
   Corinna
   Dawn
   Nikolette

My Brilliant Editing and Photoshop Assistant
   Gregg

Locations/Special Thanks to
    Austin Historical Estate Mansion
        Damon Harper
    Big Blue House
        Terry and Terresa
    Parkside House
        Dawn and Tom
    Sarasota Architectural Salvage, Sarasota FL
        Jesse White

Props and Costumes
    Players Theater for costume pieces and props

Business/Website/Marketing Assistance
    Art Aughey
    Lorenzo Emden
    Claire Seminario

Very Special Thanks For Support and Encouragement.
    Mom and Dad
    My Family and Friends
    My Facebook Community

Special acknowledgement, unfathomable gratitude and many smooches to Ashlee, Athena, Cat, Claire, Corinna, Dawn, Evfa (Supreme goddess of advice), Finnen, Gregg, Janne, Kathy, Katie, Kara C., Krista, Mickie, Scottlyn and Trish who encouraged me through this creative learning process. They were sounding boards, brain storming partners, touchstones and lifelines. Talked me off the edge when needed, brought me grown up drinks and chocolates and are my cheerleaders, you are all full of awesome. I am the luckiest art girl to have you in my world. (She Curtsies)

Follow me down the rabbit hole and through the looking glass. Put on your comfy pajamas, leave your adult cares at the door and whisper, "Curiouser and Curiouser". Bring your best crayons, colored pencils, markers and your sassy artist attitude that you had when you were five and let your adventure in Wonderland begin.

There was nothing so VERY remarkable in that; nor did Alice think it so VERY much out of the way to hear the Rabbit say to itself, `oh dear! oh dear! I shall be late!' (when she thought it over afterwards, it occurred to her that she ought to have wondered at this, but at the time it all seemed quite natural)
-Lewis Carroll

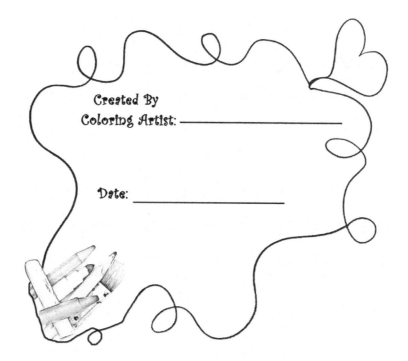

Created By
Coloring Artist: _____

Date: _____

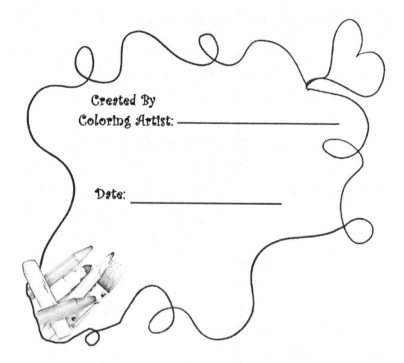

Created By
Coloring Artist: _____

Date: _____

"oh my ears and whiskers, how late it's getting!"
-White Rabbit

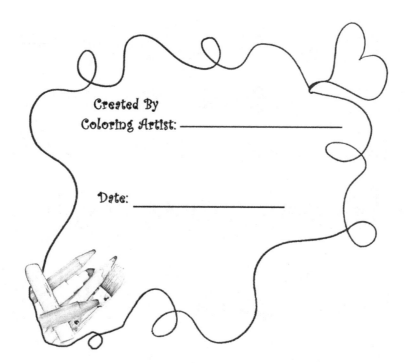

Created By
Coloring Artist: _____

Date: _____

9

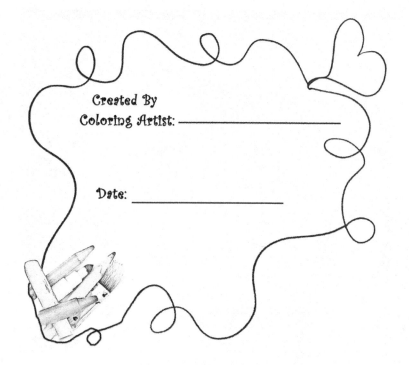

Created By
Coloring Artist: _____

Date: _____

"I - I hardly know, sir, just at present - at least I know who I WAS when I got up this morning, but I think I must have been changed several times since then." -Alice

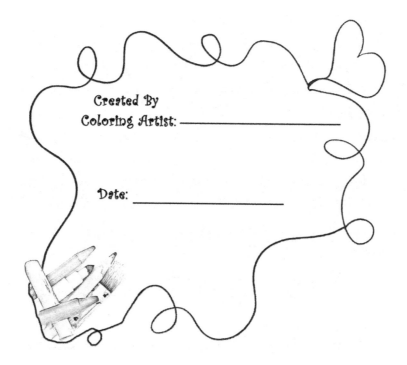

Created By
Coloring Artist: ————————————————

Date: ————————————————

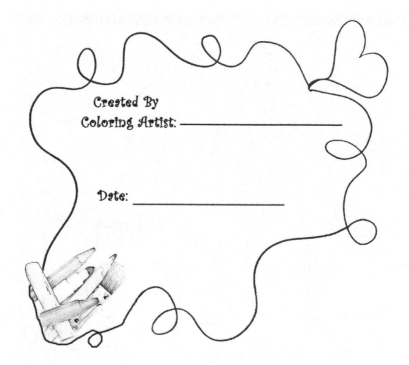

Created By
Coloring Artist: _____

Date: _____

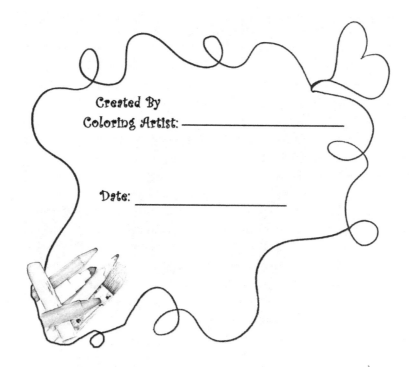

Created By
Coloring Artist: _____

Date: _____

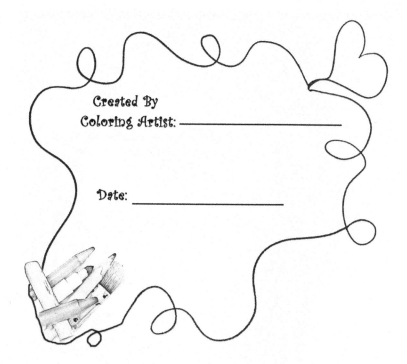

Created By
Coloring Artist: _____

Date: _____

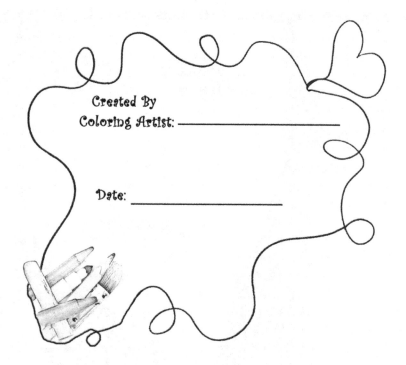

Created By
Coloring Artist: _____

Date: _____

21

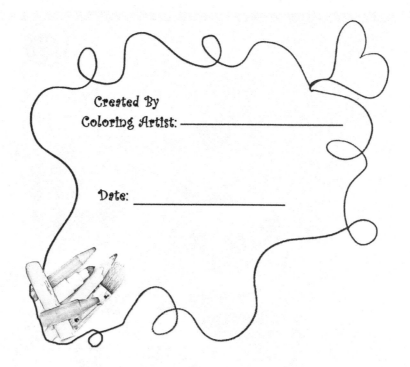

Created By
Coloring Artist: _____

Date: _____

Alice said "Would you tell me, please, which way I ought to go from here?" "That depends a good deal on where you want to get to," said the Cat.

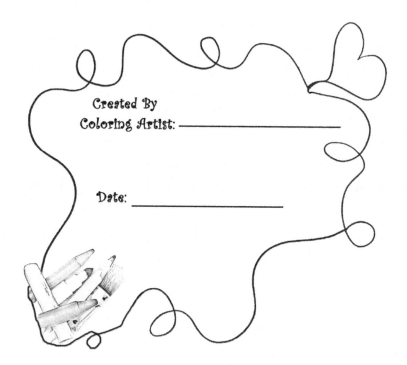

Created By
Coloring Artist: _____

Date: _____

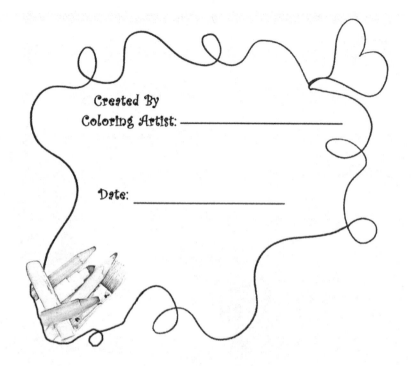

Created By
Coloring Artist: _____

Date: _____

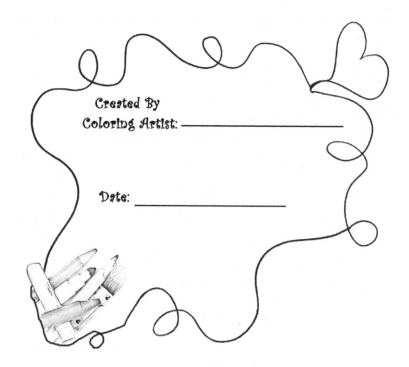

Created By
Coloring Artist: _____

Date: _____

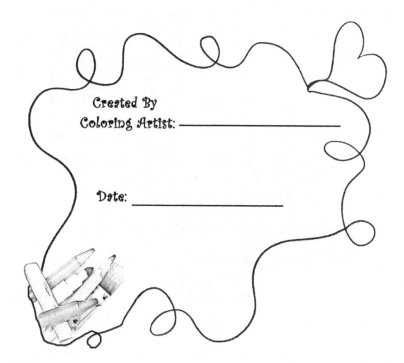

Created By
Coloring Artist: _____

Date: _____

"At any rate I'll never go THERE again!" said Alice as she picked her way through the wood. "It's the stupidest tea-party I ever was at in all my life!"

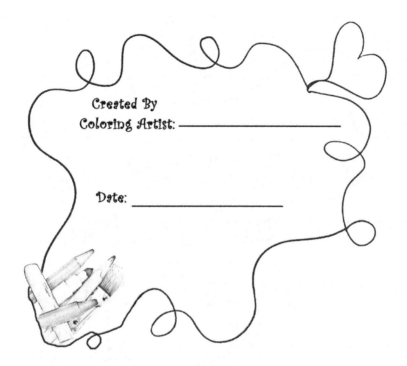

Created By
Coloring Artist: _____

Date: _____

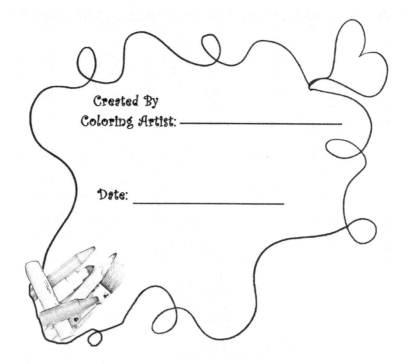

Created By
Coloring Artist: _____

Date: _____

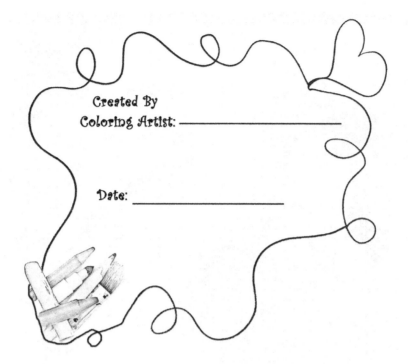

Created By
Coloring Artist: ———————————

Date: ———————————

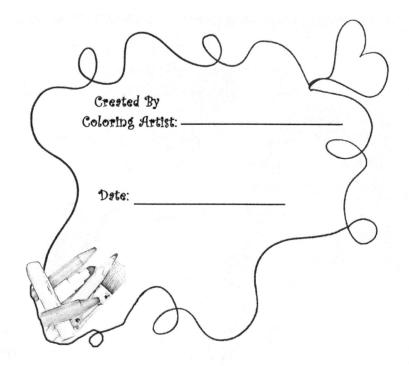

Created By
Coloring Artist: _____

Date: _____

"That begins with an M, such as mousetraps, and the moon, and the memory and muchness."

-Dormouse

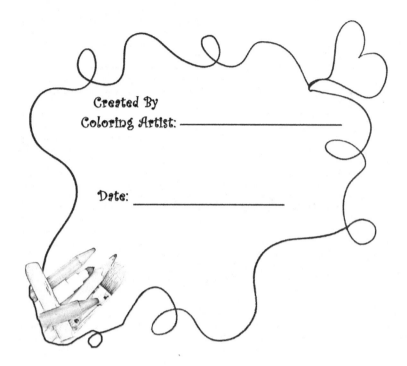

Created By
Coloring Artist: _____

Date: _____

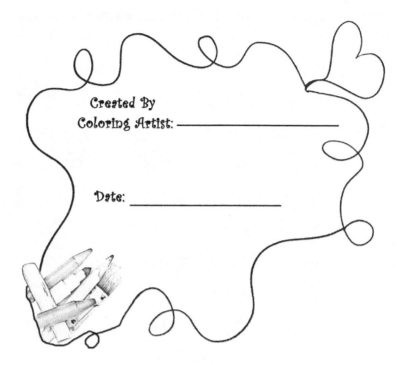

Created By
Coloring Artist: _____

Date: _____

"Take some more tea."
-March Hare

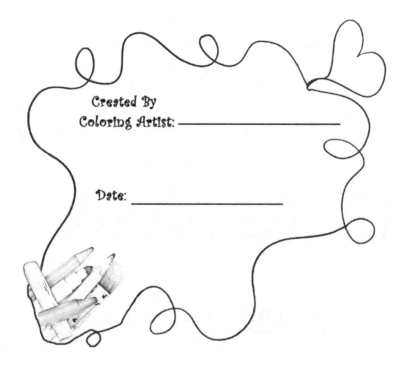

Created By
Coloring Artist: _____

Date: _____

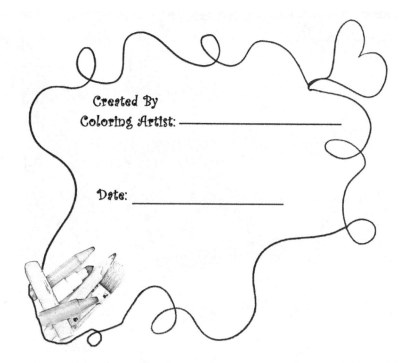

Created By
Coloring Artist: _____

Date: _____

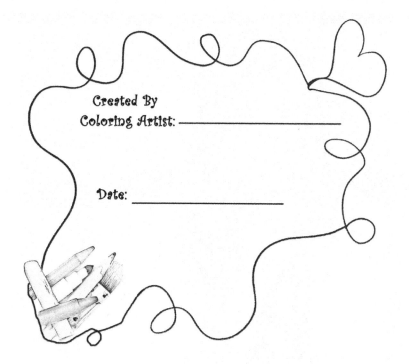

Created By
Coloring Artist: _____

Date: _____

49

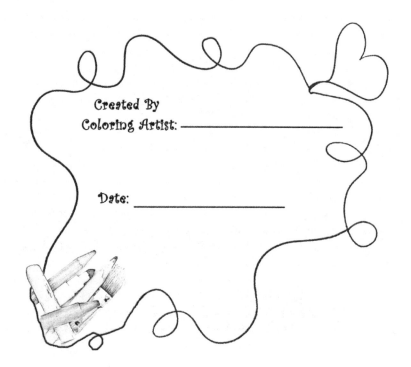

Created By
Coloring Artist: _____

Date: _____

51

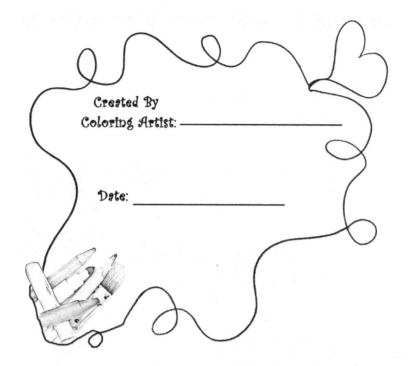

Created By
Coloring Artist: _____

Date: _____

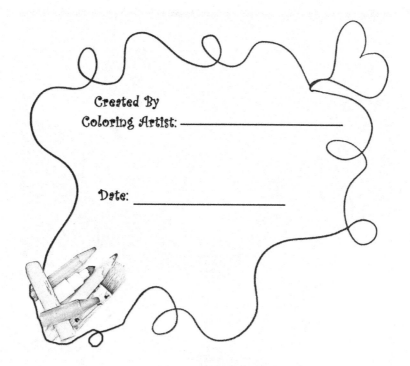

Created By
Coloring Artist: _____

Date: _____

The chief difficulty Alice found at first was managing her flamingo.

-Lewis Carroll

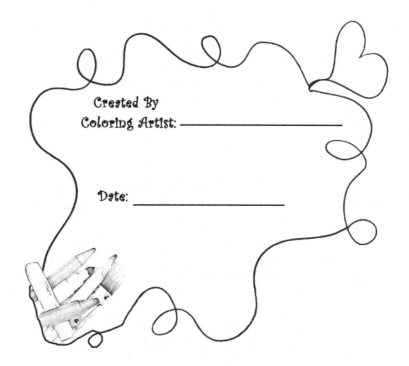

Created By
Coloring Artist: _____

Date: _____

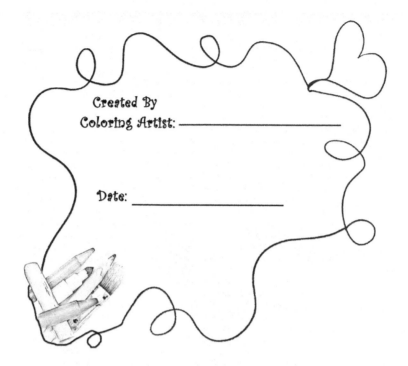

Created By
Coloring Artist: _____

Date: _____

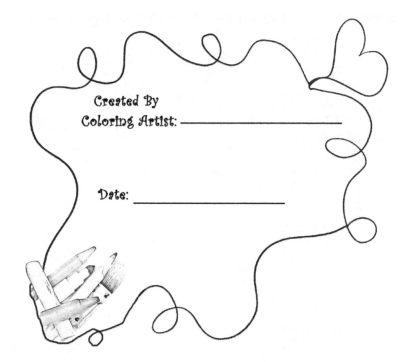

Created By
Coloring Artist: _____

Date: _____

"Why, they're only a pack of cards after all. I needn't be afraid of them."
-Alice

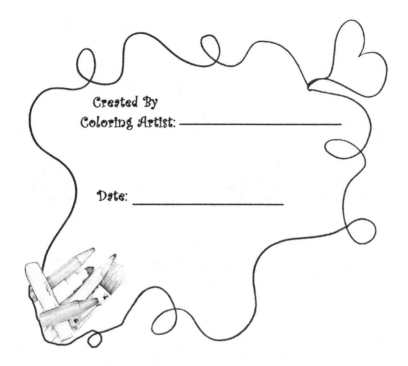

Created By
Coloring Artist: _____

Date: _____

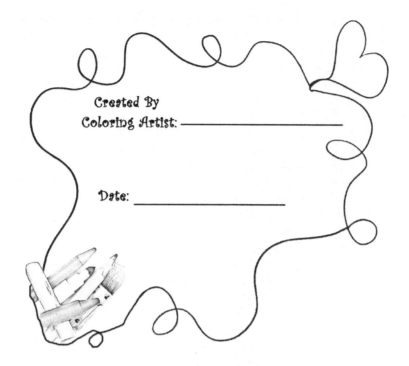

Created By
Coloring Artist: _____

Date: _____

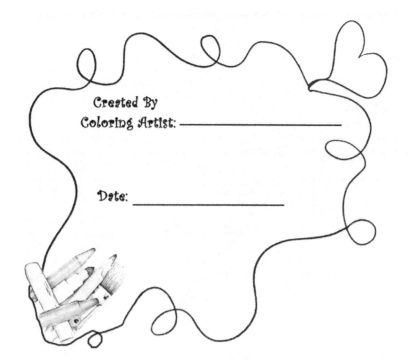

Created By
Coloring Artist: ————————————

Date: ————————————

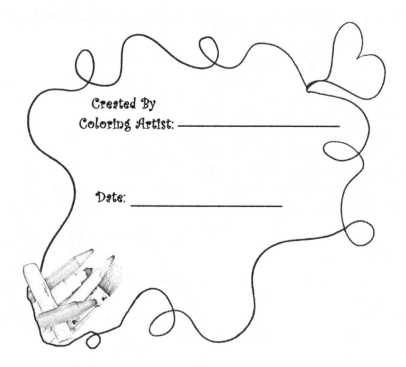

Created By
Coloring Artist: _____

Date: _____

"Off with their heads!"
-Red Queen

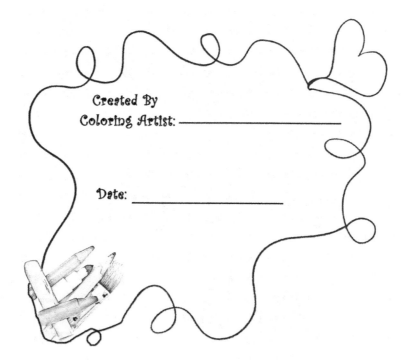

Created By
Coloring Artist: _____

Date: _____

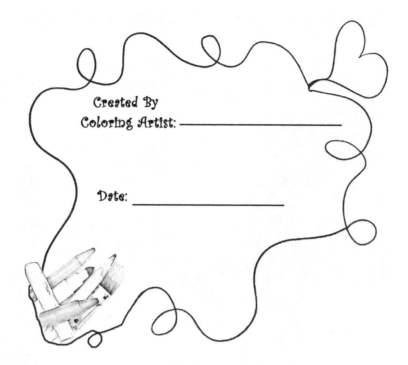

Created By
Coloring Artist: _____

Date: _____

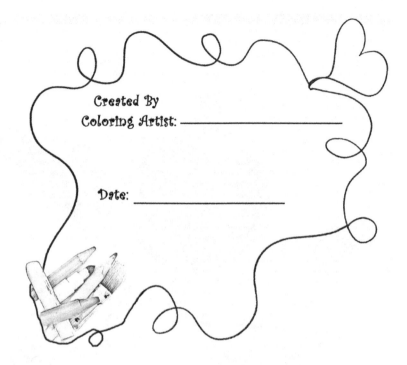

Created By
Coloring Artist: _____

Date: _____

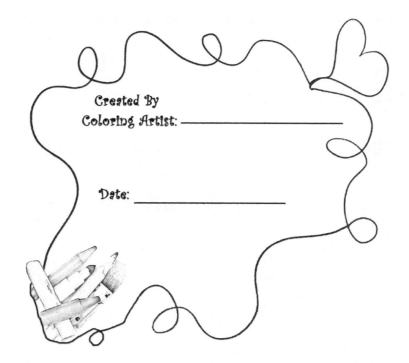

Created By
Coloring Artist: _____

Date: _____

"Once," said the Mock Turtle at last, with a deep sigh, "I was a real Turtle."

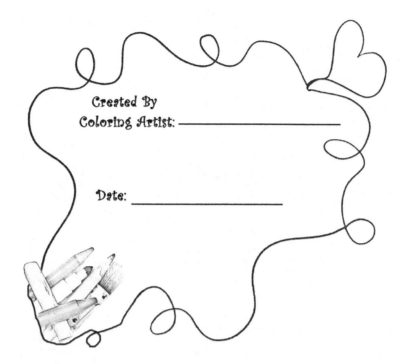

Created By
Coloring Artist: _____

Date: _____

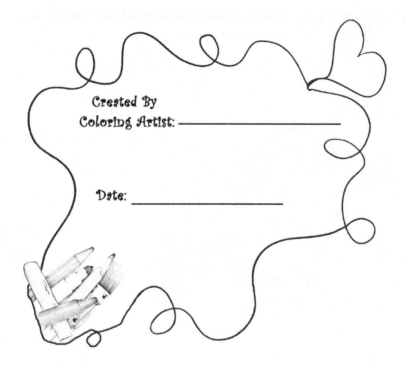

Created By
Coloring Artist: _____

Date: _____

Through the looking glass...

"Oh, Kitty! How nice would it be if only we could get through into looking-glass house!"

-Alice

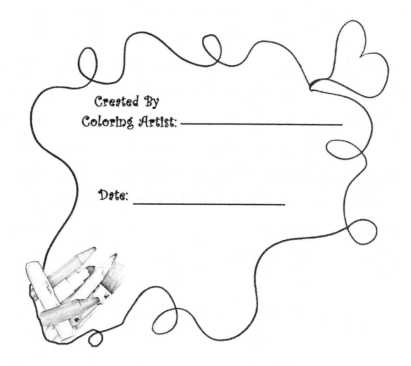

Created By
Coloring Artist: _____

Date: _____

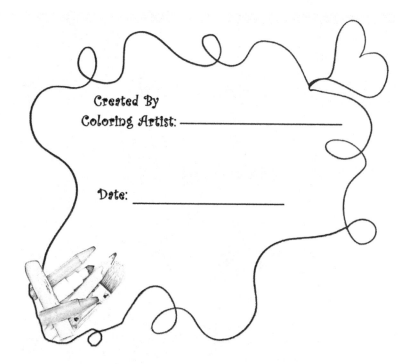

Created By
Coloring Artist: _____

Date: _____

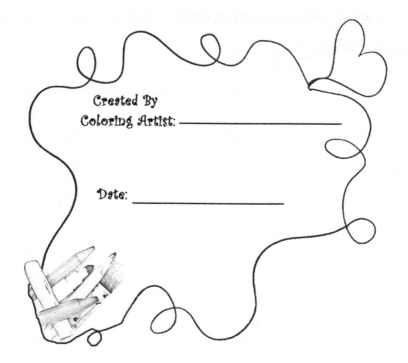

Created By
Coloring Artist: _____

Date: _____

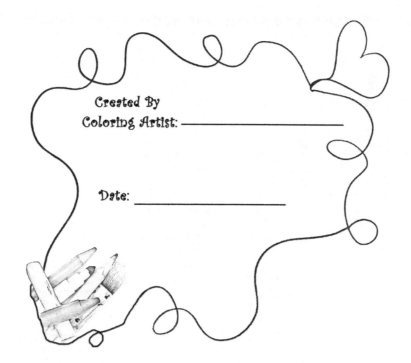

Created By
Coloring Artist: _____

Date: _____

"I know what you're thinking about," said Tweedledum: "but it isn't so, nohow." "Contrariwise," continued Tweedledee, "if it was so, it might be, and if it were so, it would be, but as it isn't, it ain't. That's logic."

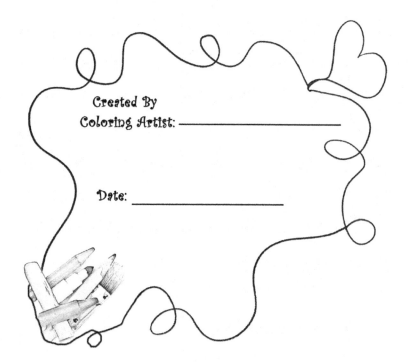

Created By
Coloring Artist: _____

Date: _____

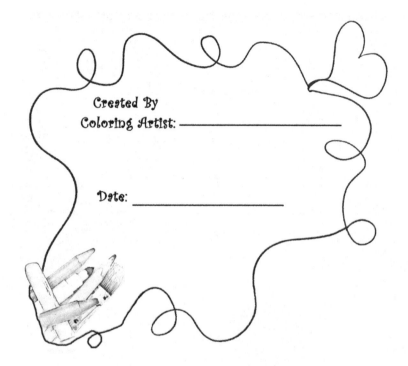

Created By
Coloring Artist: _____

Date: _____

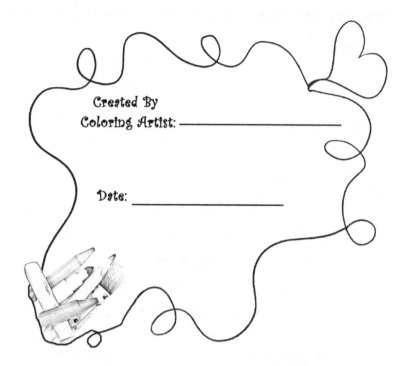

Created By
Coloring Artist: _____

Date: _____

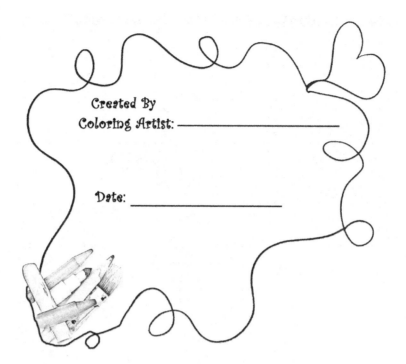

Created By
Coloring Artist: _____

Date: _____

"Why, sometimes I've believed as many as six impossible things before breakfast."
White Queen

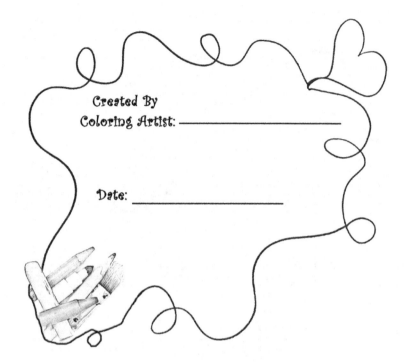

Created By
Coloring Artist: _____

Date: _____

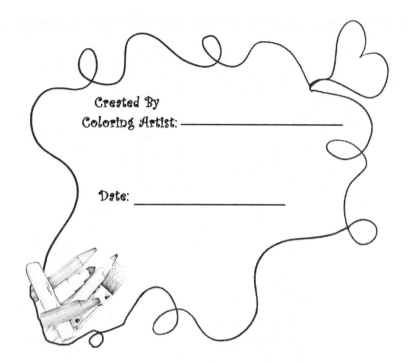

Created By
Coloring Artist: _____

Date: _____

(Alice said) in a timid voice - almost in a whisper. "And can all the flowers talk?" "As well as all can," said the Tiger-lily. "And a great deal louder."

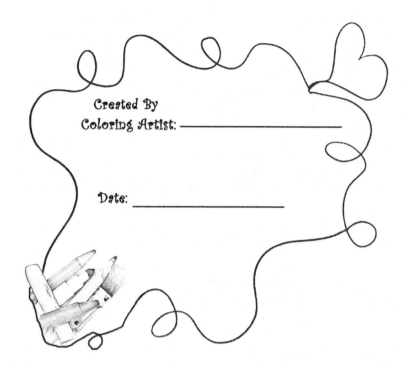

Created By
Coloring Artist: _____

Date: _____

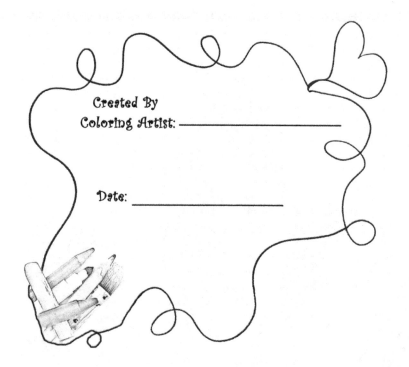

Created By
Coloring Artist: _____

Date: _____

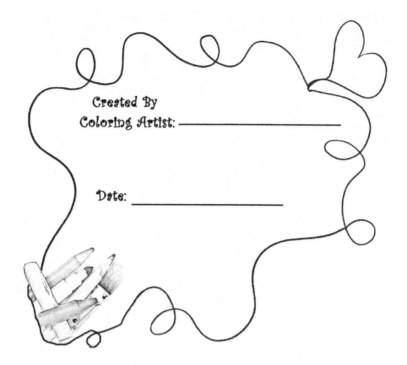

Created By
Coloring Artist: _____

Date: _____

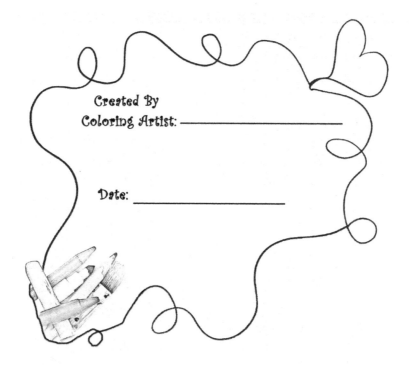

Created By
Coloring Artist: _____

Date: _____

Hush-a-by lady, in Alice's lap!
Till the feast's ready,
we've time for a nap:
When the feast's over,
we'll go to the ball
- Red Queen,
and White
Queen, and Alice,
and all!
-Lewis Carroll

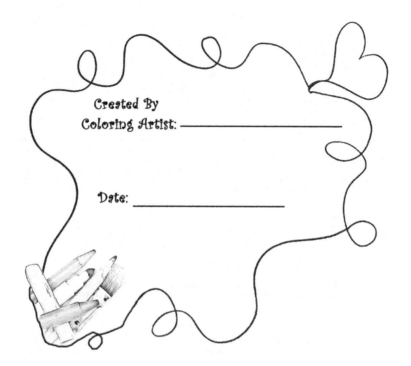

Created By
Coloring Artist: _____

Date: _____

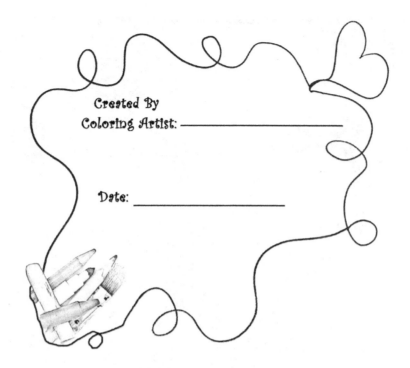

Created By
Coloring Artist: _____

Date: _____

'To the Looking-Glass world it was Alice that said, "I've a sceptre in hand, I've a crown on my head; Let the Looking-Glass creatures, whatever they be, Come and dine with the Red Queen, the White Queen, and me."'

-Alice

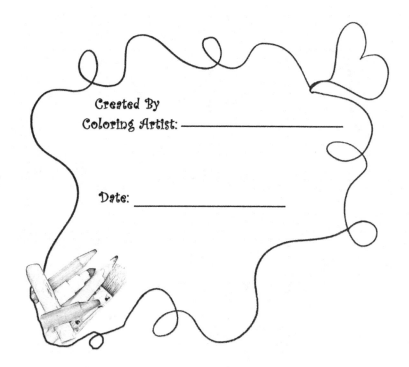

Created By
Coloring Artist: —————————————

Date: ———————————

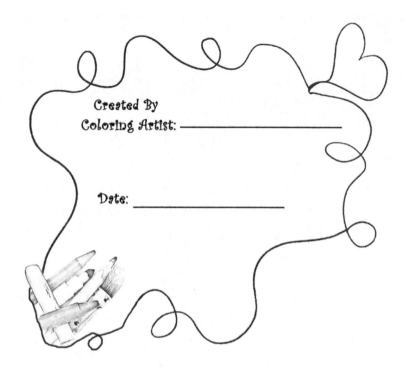

Created By
Coloring Artist: _____

Date: _____

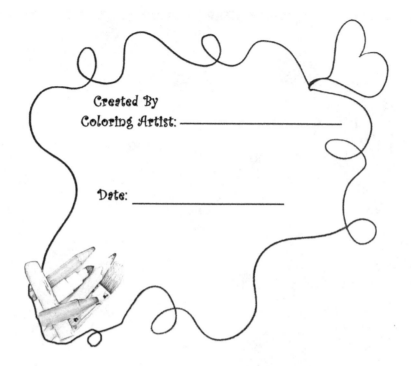

Created By
Coloring Artist: _____

Date: _____

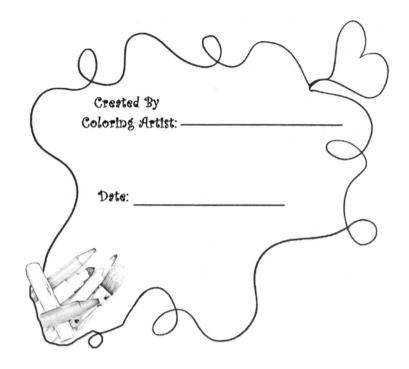

Created By
Coloring Artist: _____

Date: _____

"You woke me out of oh! Such a nice dream! And you've been along with me, Kitty - all through the Looking-Glass world. Did you know it, dear?"
-Alice

121

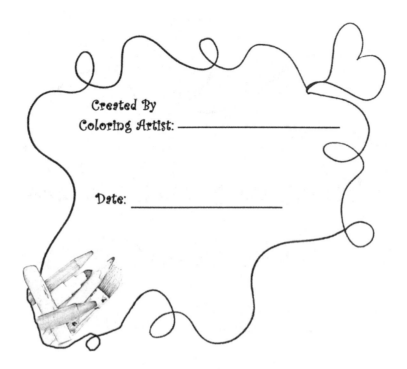

Created By
Coloring Artist: _____

Date: _____

I hope you have enjoyed my artistic adventures through Wonderland, and that it has led you to dwell in childlike belief and imagination. Also that you have delighted in the simple act of coloring, leaving you relaxed and restored. I invite you to join Alice and the rest of the Wonderland characters in my other collections of this magical story.

Shades of Alice:
Wonderland, Hats and a Looking Glass

An enchanting grayscale coloring book with a vintage photo feel. Boldly stretch your artistic wings and color Alice and many of the other characters in their travels through wonderland.

Not Your Ordinary Alice:
Wonderland, Hats and a Looking Glass

A unique small format coffee table book of my photographs that will take you on a journey with Alice and company through Wonderland as seen in my imagination.

www.TangledEnchantmentStudio.com

COLOR AND BLEED TEST PAGES

Made in the USA
Columbia, SC
08 August 2020